Beautiful
beaded jewellery

Stéphanie Bourgeois
Barbara Le Garsmeur

David & Charles

Acknowledgments

The editor and authors would like to thank:

"ENTRÉE DES FOURNISSEURS" for their warm welcome and "LA DROGUERIE" for their invaluable help.

A non-exhaustive list of suppliers of beads, buttons, ribbons and other accessories is given at the end of this book.

LAYOUT AND COVER: Agnès Frégé, Caroline Hartley

ILLUSTRATIONS: Agnès Frégé

PHOTOGRAPHY: Cactus Studio – Fabrice Besse

EDITOR: Mélanie Bauer-Giordana

CHIEF EDITOR: Catherine Franck

REVISION AND CORRECTION: Isabelle Macé

TECHNICAL CO-ORDINATORS: Nicolas Perrier and Christelle Leplard

PHOTOENGRAVING: Art Nord

A DAVID & CHARLES BOOK

First published in the UK in 2004
Originally published as *Merveilles de perles* by Dessain et Tolra, France 1999
Reprinted 2004, 2005(Twice), 2006, 2007
Copyright © Dessain et Tolra / HER 1999, 2004

Distributed in North America
by F&W Publications, Inc.
4700 East Galbraith Road
Cincinnati, OH 45236
1-800-289-0963

A catalogue record for this book is available from the British Library.

ISBN 0 7153 1797 0

Printed in China by SNP Leefung
for David & Charles
Brunel House   Newton Abbot   Devon

Visit our website at www.davidandcharles.co.uk

David & Charles books are available from all good bookshops; alternatively you can contact our Orderline on (0)1626 334555 or write to us at FREEPOST EX2110, David & Charles Direct, Newton Abbot, TQ12 4ZZ (no stamp required UK mainland).

Contents

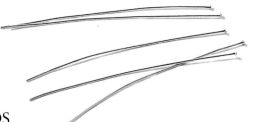

SPRUNG NECKLACE WIRE

THREADS

You will make the majority of your novelty jewellery pieces using some sort of thread or wire. It is important to choose carefully as different threads and wires can have a significant effect on the strength and end result of the jewellery.

Nylon threads are very robust. They come in a variety of colours and thicknesses; the finest nylon thread is often used for threading on small glass beads or for making knotted, cobweb-type necklaces. The thickest threads can be used in much the same way as tiger tail (see below). They should not be used for weaving with beads, however, as they are fairly stiff.

Tiger tail is a nylon-covered thin metal wire that comes in a variety of colours and thicknesses. It is one of the most robust threads available and is suitable for use with weighty beads made from glass and stone. As tiger tail is fairly stiff, it is impractical to make knots in it, so you should secure it with small metal beads, known as crimp beads, which you can crush using a pair of flat-nosed pliers (see page 6). Tiger tail is also suitable for making necklaces where the thread is visible (see Stardust, page 52).

Yarn is strong and flexible and is used for weaving and threading on small beads. It comes in a wide range of colours but is not as strong as nylon thread.

Metal wires are made either from brass (in gold or silver) or enamelled copper (in a variety of colours) and are ideal for creating more solid pieces of jewellery. They are easy to shape by hand. Although these wires are made from metal, they are fragile and should only be twisted gently.

Metal eye pins and head pins come either with a flat head (head pins) or with a looped end (eye pins) and can be found in gold, silver and copper. They are used mainly to make pendants, but can be joined together to make necklaces.

Sprung necklace wire is made of stiff circles that are generally left undecorated except for a few beads. They can also be used as bases for more intricate beadwork with metal wire (see Spiky Style, page 38).

Other materials You can choose from several other types of thread and wire, including cotton and leather thonging, string, bicycle brake wire and plastic tubing.

NYLON THREAD AND PLASTIC TUBING

TIGER TAIL

METAL WIRES

STRING

CLASPS

There are several types of clasp and it is important that you choose a clasp suited to the type of jewellery you intend to make and the weight of the finished piece.

Barrel clasps are often used in necklace-making. For practical reasons (they require two hands for fastening) you should avoid using them when making bracelets. They are not recommended for use on sprung metal wire necklaces as they have a tendency to unscrew.

Round and trigger clasps are suitable for use on all types of jewellery. They are attached to double rings and are opened by drawing back the fastening device.

Toggle clasps comprise a toggle that sits inside a ring. They are used to make bracelets and necklaces.

Press stud clasps work on the same principle as press studs and can be used in necklaces and bracelets.

Other clasps You can make your own clasp. Make a button loop from several threads at one end of the necklace and fix a bead or button at the other end. There are also plastic clasps for delicate skin, and clasps for making necklaces with several rows.

ROUND AND TRIGGER CLASPS

BARREL CLASPS

PRESS STUD CLASP

TOGGLE CLASP

PLASTIC CLASPS

CRIMP BEADS

SECURING A SINGLE WIRE OR THREAD

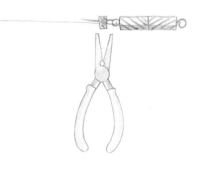

SECURING SEVERAL WIRES OR THREADS

1. THREAD THE WIRES OR THREADS INTO A CRIMP BEAD AND SQUEEZE WITH FLAT-NOSED PLIERS.

2. PLACE THE CRIMP BEAD INSIDE A BEAD TIP WITH A SMALL DAB OF GLUE.

3. ATTACH THE BEAD TIP TO YOUR CLASP USING THE END TO MAKE A RING.

END PIECES

Crimp beads are small metal beads that are used to secure wires when knotting is impractical. Use them on tiger tail and nylon thread.

Securing a wire or thread:

1. Thread on the crimp bead.

2. Thread the wire or thread through the clasp and back through the crimp bead.

3. Pull the bead tight against the clasp and crush the crimp using a pair of flat-nosed pliers.

Securing several wires or threads to a single clasp:

1. Thread the wires through a crimp bead and crush the crimp using flat-nosed pliers.

2. Place the crimp bead in a bead tip with a small amount of glue to secure.

3. Attach the bead tip to the clasp using the end to make a ring.

Bead tips are small, shell-like beads that can be closed around a knot or crimp bead for a neat finish. To make your jewellery more secure, apply a small amount of glue to the knot before closing the bead tip.

Leather crimps are used mainly for securing lengths of leather thonging on to clasps. They can also be used to secure several lengths of wire to a single clasp.

APPLY GLUE TO THE LEATHER CRIMP, PLACE THE LEATHER THONGING IN IT AND FLATTEN THE CRIMP CAREFULLY WITH FLAT-NOSED PLIERS. ATTACH THE CRIMP TO YOUR CLASP USING A JUMP RING IF NECESSARY.

LEATHER CRIMPS

RINGS

Double rings look a little like key rings and have two winds of wire. They are more robust than single rings and can support a heavier load. They are used with round or trigger clasps.

Single jump rings are broken rings that can be opened using flat-nosed pliers. They are used mainly for joining pieces together and for hanging pendants.

TOOLS

Flat-nosed pliers are used by electricians. Opt for the thinnest pliers you can find. You can use flat-nosed pliers to squeeze crimp beads and secure most end pieces.

Round-nosed pliers are used mainly for working rings, with eye pins or head pins for example. Flat-nosed and round-nosed pliers often have a cutting edge that is useful for working with eye pins, head pins and thick metal wires.

Glue helps to secure your pieces and is especially useful when working with bead tips. Ensure that you choose a slow-drying glue as it will last much longer than a fast-drying glue.

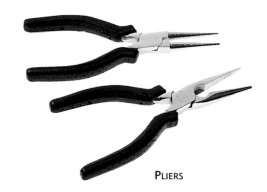

PLIERS

JUMP RINGS

BEAD TIPS AND CALOTTES

Beaded Insects

DRAGONFLY AND BUTTERFLIES

Make up the body and wings of each beaded insect separately.

Materials required

- *60cm (24in) thin wire for each section of each insect*
- *small glass beads in assorted colours*
- *hairclip or brooch mount*

For the choker

- *roughly 50cm (20in) ribbon*
- *1 button*

① To make the wings

Follow the patterns shown below and on page 10. Thread on the first row of beads and slide them to the centre of the wire. Pick up the next row of beads on one end of the wire and take the other end of the wire through, crossing inside. Pull wire tight. Continue in this way. Leave the excess wire to attach the wings to the body.

② To make the body

Follow the patterns shown below and on page 10. Start at the base (butterfly) or head (dragonfly) and follow the same process as for the wings (see step 1). To make the antennae, thread seven beads on to each wire, loop over final bead and go back through the first six beads. Twist the wire tight and trim.

③ Assembling the insect

Attach each wing to the body by twisting the excess wire on either side of a row of beads.

④ To make the brooch or hairclip

To attach the dragonfly to the brooch mount or hairclip, wind the excess metal wire around the mount and secure with a little glue. For the butterfly use a little extra wire and secure with glue.

⑤ To make the choker

Sew the small butterfly (see page 10) on to the ribbon. To fasten, sew a button at one end of the ribbon and a buttonhole decorated with beads at the other end.

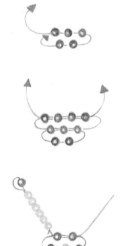

2. START WORK ON THE BUTTERFLY BODY FROM THE BASE. TO MAKE THE ANTENNAE, THREAD ON SEVEN BEADS, LOOP OVER FINAL BEAD AND GO BACK THROUGH THE REMAINING SIX BEADS.

Large Butterfly

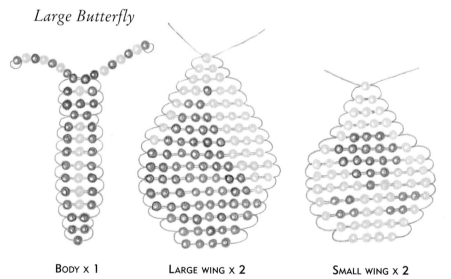

BODY X 1   LARGE WING X 2   SMALL WING X 2

Use these patterns as inspiration for your own motifs. Work out new designs on squared paper.

To make a choker, sew the butterfly to the middle of the ribbon.

Small Butterfly

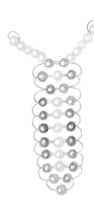

BODY X 1   LARGE WING X 2   SMALL WING X 2

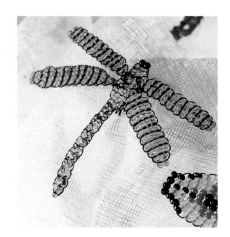

To make a dragonfly brooch or hairclip, wind the excess wire around the mount.

Dragonfly

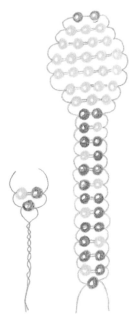

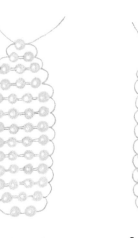

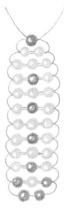

LARGE WING
x 2

SMALL WING
x 2

BODY X 1

Work the dragonfly's body starting from the head. When you have finished, twist the wires and bend them back underneath the body.

LADYBIRD NECKLACE

The ladybird is made in a similar way to the butterflies and dragonfly. It includes a loop to attach it to the necklace.

① To make the ladybird
Start by working on the body at the base, using the diagram as a guide (see page 8). When you have finished, thread on about 12 glass beads to make a loop to attach to the necklace. Twist the wires together and bend back under the body.

② To make the necklace
Thread the clasp into the centre of the nylon thread and secure with a double knot.

③ Thread two beads on each end of the nylon then cross both ends through a different coloured bead. Repeat this process until you reach the desired length.

④ Attach the ends of the wire to the other end of the clasp with a double knot. Thread 3-4cm (1¼-1½in) wire through the beads on either side of the clasp. Thread on the ladybird pendant.

1A. MAKE THE LOOP FOR THE PENDANT HERE.

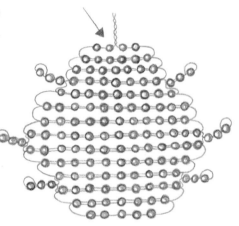

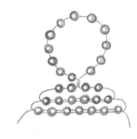

1B. THREAD THE BEADS ON THE WIRE, TWIST THE TWO ENDS TOGETHER AND BEND BACK UNDERNEATH THE HEAD.

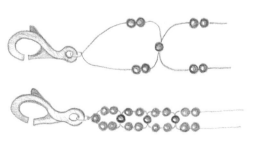

NECKLACE

Materials required
- *1.5m (4ft 11in) metal wire*
- *small glass beads in black and red*

To make the necklace
- *roughly 1.2m (4ft) nylon thread*
- *1 clasp*
- *small glass beads in black and red*

Ladybird pendant.

Bugle Band Jewellery

Materials required
For the ring
- *50cm (20in) metal wire (3mm (1/8in) in diameter)*
- *roughly 30 bugles*

Materials required
For the bracelet
- *roughly 1.5m (4ft 11in) metal wire (3mm (1/8in) in diameter)*
- *1 novelty button*
- *roughly 110 round small glass beads*
- *roughly 80 bugles*

RING

1 Thread a bugle to the centre of the wire.

2 Cross the two ends of wire inside the second bugle, then the third, and continue until you reach the desired length.

3 Assemble the ring by threading the wire back through the first two or three bugles.

You can use a small round glass bead as a spacer between the bugles, if wished.

BRACELET

1 Thread the novelty button to the centre of the wire.

2 Thread two or three round beads on each end of the wire. Cross the wires inside a bugle, a bead and another bugle (see below).

3 Use a glass bead as a spacer between each set of bugles.

4 When you reach the required length, make a button loop the size of the button you threaded on first. Cross the wires through the final bugles and then twist the wires together (see below).

Vary the space between motifs by altering the number of beads you thread on each time.

Ring

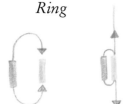

1. STARTING OFF.

2. THREADING ON THE BEADS.

3. ASSEMBLING THE RING.

Bracelet

1. STARTING OFF.

2. FIRST SET OF BUGLES.

3. THREADING ON THE BEADS.

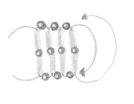

4. MAKING A BUTTON LOOP.

Buttons and Beads

Materials required

- *80cm (31¹/2in) metal wire*
- *small glass beads (3mm (¹/8in) in diameter) in assorted colours*
- *standard or novelty holed buttons, in assorted colours*
- *2 × 50cm (20in) ribbon*

① To make the necklace
Thread about fifteen small glass beads to the centre of the wire.

**② ** Thread on a button. Thread each end of wire through a button hole from the back. Thread a bead on each end, then go back through the button holes (into the same holes or into the third and fourth holes where applicable).

**③ ** Thread a few small glass beads on each wire and then another button. Space the buttons evenly. Repeat steps 2 and 3 until you reach the desired length, roughly 30cm (12in).

**④ ** Finish the end of the necklace by threading on the same number of beads as in step 1, then twist the wire together under the last button.

⑤ Fastening your necklace
Halve the lengths of ribbon and thread one length through each end of the necklace, pulling the ends through a loop of ribbon to secure. Cut the ends of the ribbon on the diagonal to prevent them fraying.

1. STARTING OFF.

2. FIRST BUTTON.

3. SPACE THE BUTTONS AT REGULAR INTERVALS.

4. FINISHING THE NECKLACE.

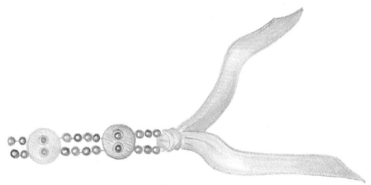

5. FASTENING THE NECKLACE.

Intertwined Flowers

Materials required
For the bracelet

- *1m (39in) nylon thread*
- *small glass beads*
- *roughly 30 faceted beads (0.6cm (¹/₄in) in diameter)*
- *12 faceted beads (3mm (¹/₈in) in diameter) or novelty small glass beads*
- *1 novelty button*

Materials required
For the necklace

- *roughly 2m (6ft 7in) nylon thread*
- *2 fairly weighty beads or droplet beads*
- *small glass beads*
- *faceted beads (0.6cm (¹/₄in) and 3mm (¹/₈in) in diameter) in assorted colours*

BRACELET

1 Thread fifteen small glass beads to the centre of the thread. Thread a large faceted bead on to each end.

2 Cross the two threads inside a small faceted bead: this will act as the centre of the flower. Thread a large faceted bead on each end.

3 Repeat this process, threading five small glass beads on each end, between flowers.

4 To finish the bracelet, attach a button with a double knot and take 3cm (1¹/₄in) thread back through the beads on each side.

Faceted beads

1. STARTING OFF.

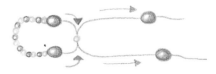

2. FIRST FLOWER.

3. AND 4. THREADING ON THE BEADS AND FINISHING OFF THE BRACELET.

DROPLET NECKLACE

1 Thread a droplet bead to the centre of the thread. Knot it, then follow the instructions for the bracelet until you reach the desired length, roughly 1.2m (4ft).

2 Secure the second large bead with a knot at the other end and take 3cm (1¹/₄in) thread back through the beads on each side.

1A. STARTING OFF.

1B. FIRST FLOWER.

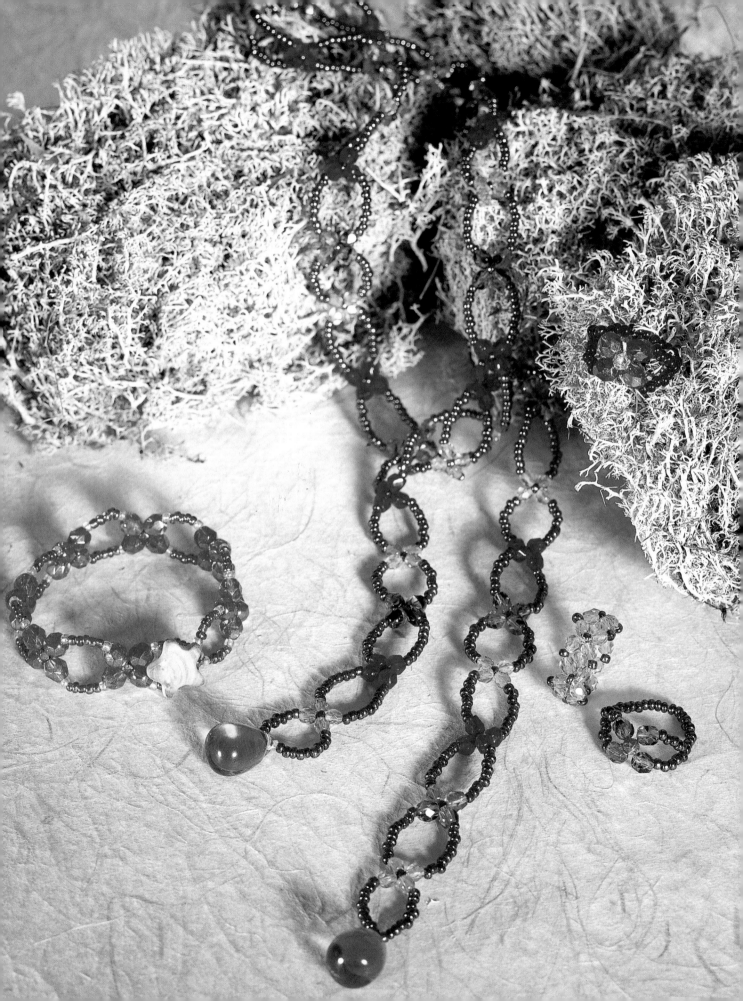

Materials required

- *roughly 30cm (11³/₄in) nylon thread*
- *small glass beads*
- *faceted beads (3mm (¹/₈in) in diameter)*

GREEN RING

1 Thread a small glass bead to the centre of the thread. Add a faceted bead, a small glass bead and another faceted bead on each end and cross the threads inside another small glass bead.

2 Repeat this process until you have the required length. Join the two ends together with a double knot and thread the ends back through several beads.

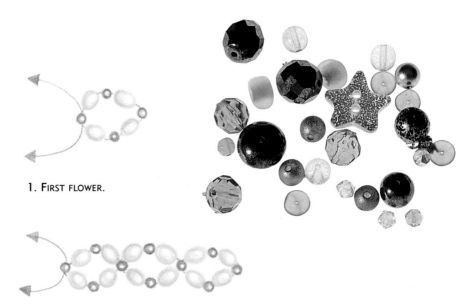

You can make this pretty ring using any leftover beads. Vary the colours to achieve different results.

1. FIRST FLOWER.

2. THREADING ON THE BEADS.

SINGLE FLOWER RING

This ring has a beaded band and a single flower design.

1 Halve the thread and thread five or six small glass beads on the doubled thread. Separate the two thread ends and thread three small glass beads and one faceted bead on each end, then cross the two ends inside a small glass bead.

2 Thread one faceted bead and three small glass beads on each end, then bring the threads together again and thread on another five or six small glass beads. Tie the ends together with a double knot and thread them back through several beads.

To prevent the beads from falling off, tie a fairly loose double knot at the start of the thread.

Materials required
- *roughly 30cm (11¾in) nylon thread*
- *small glass beads*
- *4 faceted beads*

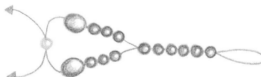

1. STARTING OFF.

2. FINISHED MOTIF.

Adjust the number of beads used in this simple ring design to ensure an exact fit for your finger.

Lacy Bead Designs

BRACELET AND RING

Materials required

- *roughly 60cm (24in) yarn for a bracelet, 20cm (8in) for a ring*
- *small glass beads, in assorted colours*
- *1 clasp for the bracelet*
- *glue*

① To make the bracelet
Attach a clasp at one end of the thread with a double knot.

② Thread on six beads in the same colour, then go back through the first bead to make a loop. Tighten against the clasp.

③ To make the centre of the flower, thread on a bead in a contrasting colour and go back through the fourth bead to secure.

④ Repeat steps 2 and 3, varying the colours as you go until you reach the required length. Tighten the flowers against each other as you work.

⑤ Tie to the other part of the clasp with a double knot, thread some thread back through several beads. Apply a dab of glue to the knot.

⑥ To make the ring
Follow the instructions for the bracelet (see steps 2 to 4), but simply tie the two ends together with a double knot.

1. and 2. ATTACHING THE CLASP AND THREADING ON THE FIRST FLOWER.

3. CENTRE OF THE FIRST FLOWER.

4. THREADING ON THE BEADS.

WOVEN NECKLACE

Materials required

- *roughly 4.5m (14ft 9in) yarn for a choker*
- *small glass beads, in assorted colours*
- *small novelty beads*
- *glue*

➊ **The first row**

Thread on a bead to secure the work roughly 20cm (8in) from the end of the yarn. Thread on a blue bead, a green/yellow bead, two turquoise beads, one green/yellow bead, two turquoise beads, one blue bead, two turquoise beads, a green/yellow bead, two turquoise beads, one blue bead and four green/yellow beads.

➋ **The second row**

Work in the opposite direction, going back through the first green/yellow bead in the group of four and then through the next blue bead. Thread on two turquoise beads, a green/yellow bead and two turquoise beads and then go into the blue bead on the

first row. Next, thread on two turquoise beads, one green/yellow bead and two more turquoise beads and go through the green and blue beads at the start of the first row.

➌ **The third row**

Thread on three turquoise beads, one blue bead, one green/yellow bead and two turquoise beads and go through the green/yellow bead on the previous row. Thread on two turquoise beads, one blue bead and two turquoise beads and go into the green/yellow bead on the previous row. Thread on two turquoise beads, one blue bead, one novelty bead and a green/yellow bead.

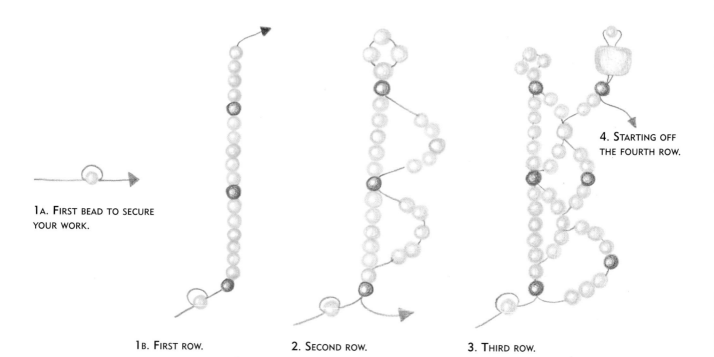

1A. FIRST BEAD TO SECURE YOUR WORK.

1B. FIRST ROW.

2. SECOND ROW.

3. THIRD ROW.

4. STARTING OFF THE FOURTH ROW.

❹ The other rows

Repeat steps 2 and 3, alternating between a group of small glass beads and a novelty bead for your pendants as many times as necessary.

❺ The clasp

Finish off the necklace by threading on some small glass beads to make a button loop the size of the novelty beads. Take the yarn back through some beads and tie around the necklace with a double knot. Remove the bead you used to secure the work at the other end of the necklace, and thread on four small glass beads and a novelty bead. Repeat three times, then tie a double knot and take some thread back through several beads. Add a dab of glue to the knots.

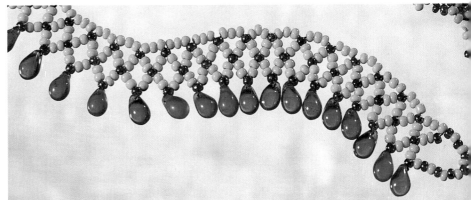

Above (top): Woven Necklace.
Above (bottom): a more simple weave using droplet pendants. This bracelet was worked in the same way but the size of the design has been reduced.

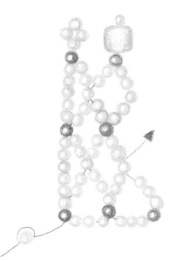

4. STARTING OFF THE FIFTH ROW.   5A. BUTTON LOOP.   5B. BEADS FOR THE FASTENING.

Multicolour Charms

Materials required

- *80cm (32in) yarn for a necklace, 40cm (16in) for a bracelet*
- *small glass beads (3mm (¹/₈in) in diameter), in assorted colours*
- *novelty beads in assorted colours*
- *2 bead tips*
- *glue*
- *1 clasp (avoid using barrel clasps to make bracelets)*

❶ To make the central pendant
Start by threading a small glass bead to the centre of your thread, then pass the two ends of thread through one or more beads to make the central pendant.

❷ To make the other pendants
Continue working with both ends of thread. Thread between five and ten small glass beads on each end, plus a novelty bead and another small glass bead, then go back into the novelty bead and a glass bead. Repeat this process until you have the required length.

❸ The clasp
Tie a double knot at each end of the bracelet or necklace and place inside a bead tip. Add a dab of glue. Attach the bead tips to the clasp.

1. CENTRAL PENDANT.

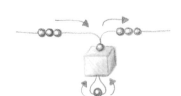

2. OTHER PENDANTS.

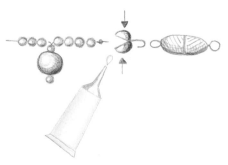

3. ASSEMBLING THE BEAD TIP AND CLASP.

Safety Pin Bracelets

Use safety pins of similar size and length for an even and secure finish.

Materials required
- *30 to 60 safety pins*
- *assorted novelty beads and buttons, in assorted colours*
- *flat-nosed pliers*
- *50cm (20in) hat elastic*
- *glue*

❶ Making up the safety pins
Thread the beads on the safety pins. If you intend to create a design, bear in mind that the safety pins will be assembled head to tail.

❷
Gently crush the heads of the safety pins closed using the flat-nosed pliers.

❸ Assembling the bracelet
Cut the elastic in half. Thread the pins on the two lengths of elastic head to tail, going through the ring of one safety pin then through the head of the next. If you are using large beads on the safety pins, use a small glass bead as a spacer between each one.

❹
Tie the elastic together at the required length and apply a dab of glue to the knot. Hide the knot under a bead.

1. THREAD THE BEADS ON TO THE PINS.

2. CRUSH THE HEADS WITH FLAT-NOSED PLIERS.

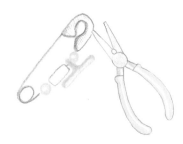

3. IF YOU ARE USING LARGE BEADS INSERT A SMALL GLASS BEAD BETWEEN THE SAFETY PINS.

4. SECURE THE KNOTS WITH A DAB OF GLUE.

Geometric Designs

BRACELET AND RING

Materials required

- *60cm (24in) tiger tail*
- *about 10 eye pins*
- *small glass beads in assorted colours*
- *several novelty beads*
- *round-nosed pliers*
- *crimp beads*
- *flat-nosed pliers*
- *wire cutters*

1. PREPARE THE EYE PINS.

① To make the bracelet
Decide on two bead patterns of different lengths to go on the eye pins and thread them on. Trim the eye pins, leaving an excess of 1cm (³⁄₈in) and make a loop on each one using round-nosed pliers.

**② ** Thread a small glass bead in the centre of your tiger tail, thread the two ends of the tiger tail through the novelty bead you will use to fasten the bracelet and then through another small glass bead.

**③ ** Separate the two lengths of tiger tail and thread six small glass beads on each end, then thread them through the rings on the longest eye pin. Add six more beads then the shorter eye pin design. Repeat, alternating long and short eye pins with glass beads, until you reach the required length.

**④ ** Thread several beads on each end of the tiger tail then thread the two ends through a crimp bead and thread on more beads to make a button loop the size of the bead you are using to fasten the bracelet. Thread the ends back through the crimp bead and into several beads. Crush the crimp using the flat-nosed pliers.

⑤ To make the ring
Work in the same way, using one design on much shorter eye pins and separating them with a single glass bead. Bring the ends of the tiger tail together by threading them through two crimp beads. Crush the crimps without leaving any slack.

2. BEAD TO FASTEN BRACELET.

3A. FIRST MOTIF.

5A. MAKING THE RING.

3B. THREADING ON THE BEADS.

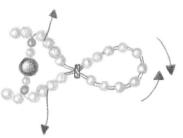

4. MAKING THE BUTTON LOOP.

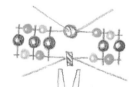

5B. ASSEMBLING THE RING.

DROP NECKLACE WITH BEADED PANEL

Materials required

- *1m (39in) thin tiger tail*
- *about 20 eye pins*
- *small glass beads, in assorted colours*
- *several novelty beads*
- *wire cutters*
- *round-nosed pliers*
- *crimp beads*
- *flat-nosed pliers*

① Preparing the eye pins
Thread the beads on the eye pins, trim 1cm (³/8in) above the beads and form a loop at the end of each eye pin using the round-nosed pliers.

② To make the necklace
Thread about 60cm (24in) small glass beads on the tiger tail.

③ Beaded panel
Place an eye pin on the two ends of the tiger tail, then thread a small glass bead on each end. Thread on another eye pin and repeat this process until you reach the desired length.

④ Finish by threading roughly 5cm (2in) small glass beads, a crimp bead, a novelty bead and another small glass bead on each end of the tiger tail. Go back through the novelty bead, the crimp bead and a few small glass beads. Tighten the tiger tail to ensure there is no slack and crush the crimp bead using flat-nosed pliers.

Prepare the design for the beaded panel on squared paper before you start work, and ensure as you go along that the eye pins are exactly the same length.

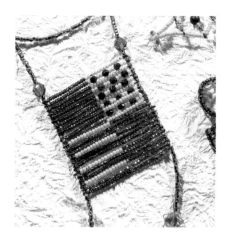

3. STARTING OFF THE BEADED PANEL.

4. FINISHING OFF.

PENDANT

❶ Preparing the eye pins

Work out a design for the pendant on squared paper before starting. Thread the beads on the eye pins, cut the pins 1cm (³/₈in) above the beads and make a loop using the round-nosed pliers.

Prepare all the eye pins, ensuring they are all the same length. Leave two eye pins without beads to assemble the pendant.

❷ Assembly

Link each end of a beaded eye pin to an eye pin without beads by opening the eye and joining the rings together.

❸ Thread one or two small glass beads on each empty eye pin, thread on another beaded eye pin and repeat the pattern until you reach the penultimate eye pin.

❹ Attach the final eye pin in the same way as you did the first (see step 2).

❺ Attach the jump ring between two eye pins on the upper row of the pendant and thread it on a chain or small glass bead necklace.

❻ Attaching the droplet beads

Thread a novelty bead on a head pin. Form a closed ring at the top and hang from the main pendant. Repeat for the required number of droplet beads.

2. FIRST EYE PIN.

3. THREADING ON THE EYE PINS.

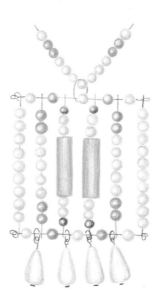

5. AND 6. THE FINISHED PENDANT.

Materials required

- *about 10 eye pins*
- *small glass beads and novelty beads, in assorted colours*
- *wire cutters*
- *round-nosed pliers*
- *1 jump ring*
- *flat-nosed pliers*
- *4 head pins*
- *4 droplet beads*

To finish, add some droplet beads, threading them on to head pins and hanging from the bottom of the pendant.

Drops of Sunlight

Materials required

- *1.5m (4ft 11in) metal wire*
- *small glass beads (0.6cm (1/4in) in diameter) or novelty beads, in assorted colours*
- *1 clasp (avoid using barrel clasps)*

① Start from the centre of the necklace. Thread the first bead into the centre of the wire. Gently twist the ends of the wire together above the bead for 4cm (1 5/8in).

② Work on one half of the necklace, then repeat the pattern on the other half. Thread on the second bead about 5cm (2in) from the first, and gently twist the wire above it for 2–3 cm (3/4–1 1/4in). Repeat this process, varying the short and long drops, until you have the required length.

③ Thread the wire into the clasps, then wind some excess around the end of the necklace to secure.

1. TURN THE BEAD AROUND ON ITSELF TO TWIST THE WIRE.

2. SPACE THE BEADS AT REGULAR INTERVALS ALONG YOUR NECKLACE.

3. WIND THE EXCESS WIRE AROUND ITSELF TO SECURE THE CLASP.

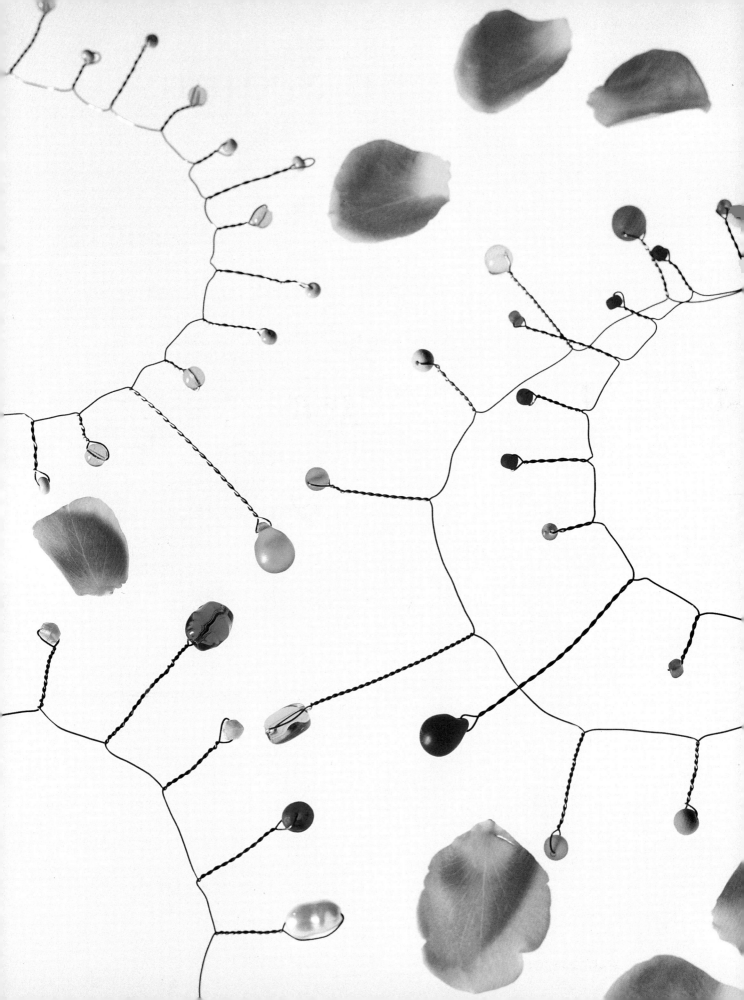

Beads and Sequins

To make this necklace you will need between three and five lengths of wire and a dozen large novelty beads that are able to contain all the wires.

Materials required

- *1m (39in) metal wire for each necklace row*
- *novelty beads, in assorted colours*
- *sequins*

❶ To make the necklace
Start at the centre of the necklace by threading all the wires through a single bead. Bend the wire up, then turn the bead on itself twice to secure.

❷ Work with both ends of the wire at the same time, threading a novelty bead or a group of sequins on to each length of wire.

❸ Repeat steps 1 and 2 every 5cm (2in) until you reach the desired length.

❹ Assembling the clasp
At one end of the necklace thread all the wires through a bead then wind them around the end of the necklace to secure. At the other end, gently twist the wires to make a button loop the size of the chosen bead.

1. TWIST THE FIRST BEAD AROUND ON ITSELF IN THE MIDDLE OF THE NECKLACE.

2. WORK ALONG EACH SIDE OF THE NECKLACE.

3. LEAVE 5CM (2IN) BETWEEN EACH OF THE LARGE BEADS.

4. MAKE THE CLASP FROM A BEAD AND A BUTTON LOOP MADE FROM TWISTED WIRE.

Bead Cascades

A necklace and bracelet are made using the same technique.

Materials required
- *beads in assorted colours*
- *1m (39in) metal wire for each necklace row, 40cm (16in) for each bracelet row*
- *2 leather crimps*
- *1 clasp*
- *2 jump rings*
- *flat-nosed pliers*

1 To make a single row
Take a length of wire, thread a fairly large bead (to fasten) into the centre and turn the bead on itself to gently twist the wire over 2–3cm (3/4–1 1/4in).

2 Thread another bead on to one length of wire then gently twist the wires together over 2–3cm (3/4–1 1/4in). Repeat this process until you reach the required length.

3 Make a button loop the size of the starting bead using the remaining wire, then wind the ends around the end of the necklace to secure.

4 To make several rows
If the starting bead is wide enough, thread all the lengths of wire through it then work the wires in pairs in the same way as for a single row.

5 Alternatively, make up each row separately then join at the ends using a leather crimp and a dab of glue. Crush the crimp at each end of the necklace using flat-nosed pliers and attach a clasp.

1. FIRST BEAD.

2. THREADING ON THE BEADS.

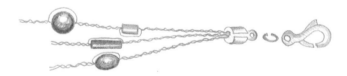

5. ASSEMBLING THE CLASP ON MULTI-ROW NECKLACES AND BRACELETS.

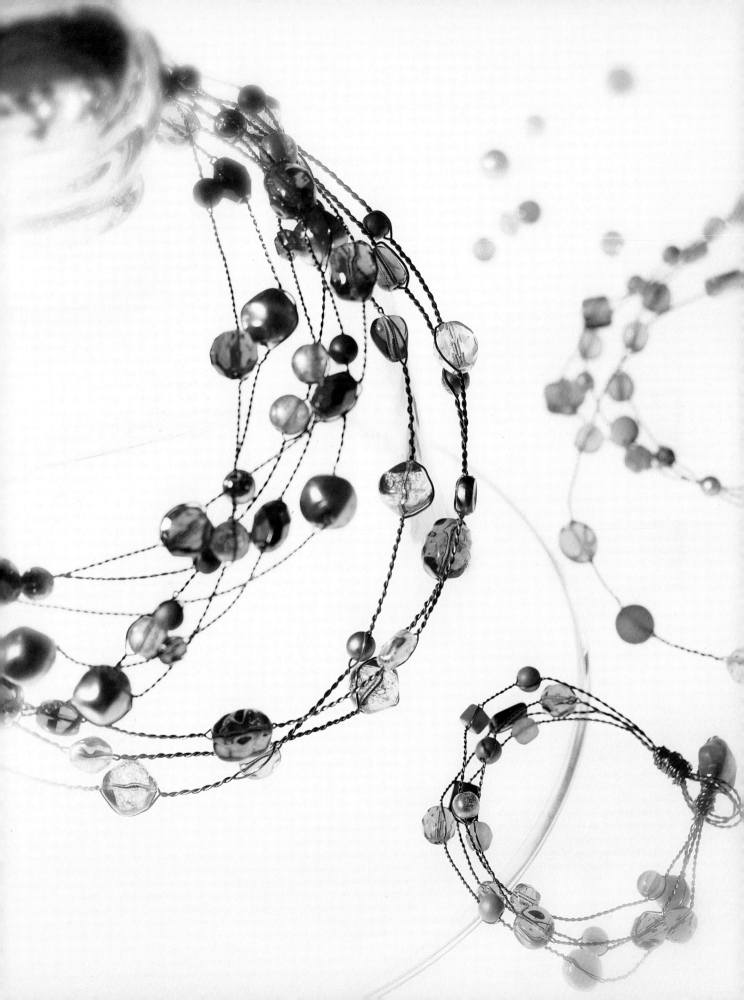

Spiky Style

NECKLACE AND HEADBAND

A clever item of jewellery which you can use as a necklace or headband.

Materials required
- *5m (16ft 5in) metal wire*
- *wire cutters*
- *1 sprung metal necklace wire or 1 headband base*
- *novelty beads and small glass beads in assorted colours*
- *glue*

1A. WIND THE WIRE AROUND THE SPRUNG NECKLACE OR HEADBAND.

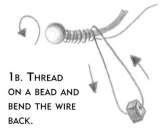

1B. THREAD ON A BEAD AND BEND THE WIRE BACK.

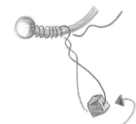

1C. TWIST THE WIRE BY TURNING THE BEAD ON ITSELF.

① Cut the metal wire in half or into three pieces to make it easier to work with. Start at one end of the sprung necklace or headband and wind the metal wire tightly around the base three or four times. Thread a novelty bead on to the metal wire leaving a 3cm (1¼in) drop. Gently twist the wire by turning the bead around on itself.

② Repeat step 1, alternating between small glass beads and novelty beads, and varying the length of drop if desired, until you reach the other end of the necklace or headband. Keep the wire tight at each end and apply a dab of glue to secure.

2. SPACE THE BEADS EVENLY, VARYING THE LENGTH OF DROP, IF DESIRED.

HAIRCLIP

Materials required
- *2–3m (6ft 7in–9ft 10in) metal wire*
- *novelty beads*
- *1 hairclip mount*

① Use the same technique as the necklace, winding the wire around the upper part of the hairclip and threading on beads as you work.

② Secure the ends of the wire in the holes at each end of the hairclip.

1A. STARTING OFF.

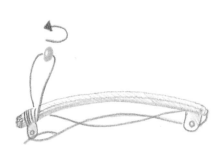

1B. FIRST BEAD.

Crazy Bead Creations

Materials required

- *1.5m (4ft 11in) metal wire for each necklace row, 60cm (24in) for each bracelet row*
- *novelty beads, in assorted colours*
- *1 larger sized bead with a large opening*

① Preparing the rows

Divide the beads up into as many piles as you have rows, then make up each row separately. Thread several beads on to the wire and bend the wire to create a zigzag pattern. Position a bead every two or three curves.

②

Continue all the way along the row, then make up the remaining rows using the same technique.

③ Assembly

Twist the ends of all the wire rows together. Thread the large bead on one end of the bracelet or necklace, bend back the excess wire and wind it around the wires to secure. At the other end, make a button loop the size of your chosen bead. Wind the ends around the end of the necklace to secure.

④ Finishing touches

Bend the necklace with your hands, intertwining the wires to make the necklace or bracelet the correct size.

1. THREADING ON THE BEADS.

3A. ATTACHING THE BEAD CLASP.

3B. MAKING THE BUTTON LOOP.

Delicate Droplets

Materials required

- *roughly 50cm (20in) thick nylon thread*
- *crimp beads*
- *novelty beads, small and large glass beads, in assorted colours*
- *flat-nosed pliers*
- *glue*
- *2 bead tips*
- *1 clasp*
- *roughly 2m (6ft 7in) fine nylon thread*

① Main necklace

Thread a crimp bead, two beads and another crimp bead on to the thick nylon thread and crush the crimps with the flat-nosed pliers. Space the pairs of beads roughly 2cm (3/4in) apart.

② When you are happy with the length of the necklace, crush a crimp bead at each end and enclose each bead in a bead tip with a dab of glue. Attach the bead tips to the clasp.

③ Pendants

Cut the fine nylon thread into 10–25cm (4–10in) lengths. Halve a length of thread and drape between the beads in one of the necklace 'pairs'. Thread both ends of this thread through a crimp bead. Push the crimp up to the main necklace and crush. Do the same for all of the pendants, starting at the front of the necklace.

④ Thread a bead on each hanging thread and secure by crushing a crimp bead at the end of the thread.

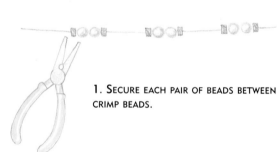

1. SECURE EACH PAIR OF BEADS BETWEEN CRIMP BEADS.

2. END OF MAIN NECKLACE.

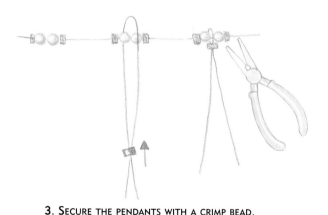

3. SECURE THE PENDANTS WITH A CRIMP BEAD.

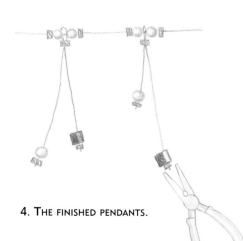

4. THE FINISHED PENDANTS.

Cobweb Necklace

To make this necklace you will need at least five lengths of thread. Prepare each row separately, ensuring the necklace is evenly balanced.

Materials required
- *roughly 1.5m (4ft 11in) nylon thread for each necklace row*
- *novelty beads, small glass beads and sequins in assorted colours*
- *glue*
- *2 bead tips*
- *1 clasp*

① Preparing the rows
Divide the beads up into as many piles as you want rows. Thread the beads on to one length of nylon, thread one by one (or in pairs or threes for small glass beads) and, taking the two ends of the thread, tie a double knot over each one. Space the beads roughly 2cm ($^3/_4$in) apart.

②
Repeat step 1 until you reach the desired length. Make up all of the rows using the same technique.

③ Assembly
Tie the rows together at both ends with a tight knot, add a dab of glue and place in the bead tips. Attach the bead tips to the clasps.

1. SECURE EACH BEAD WITH A DOUBLE KNOT.

2. SPACE THE BEADS AT REGULAR INTERVALS.

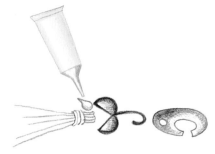

3. APPLY GLUE TO THE KNOT BEFORE PLACING IT INSIDE THE BEAD TIP.

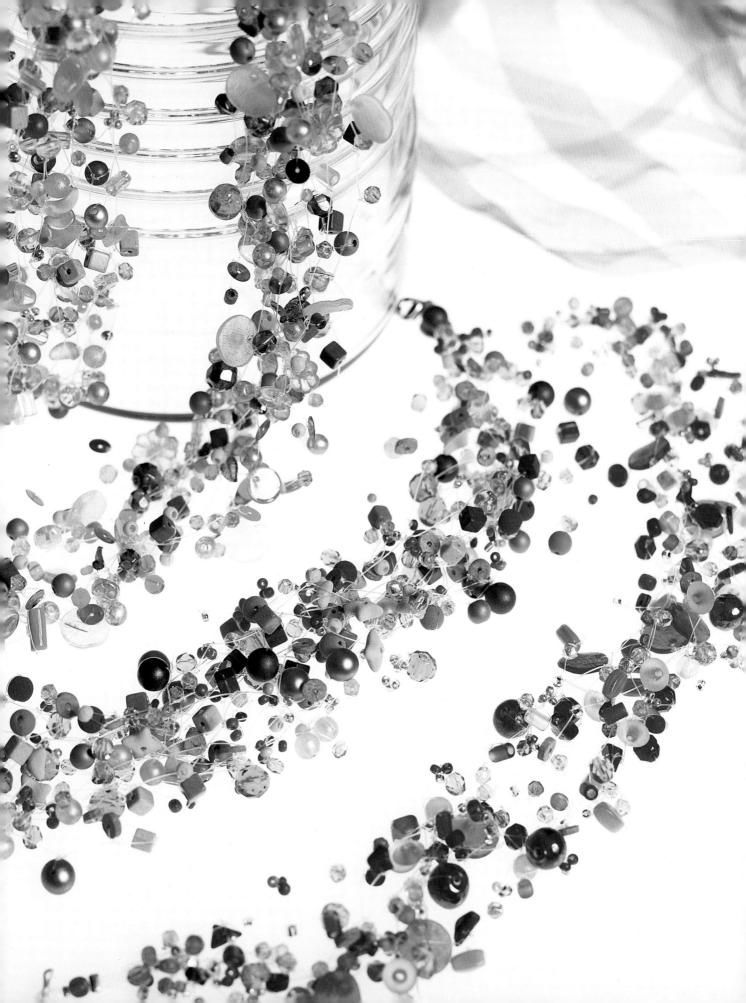

Bugle Fanfare

You will need at least three rows to make up this necklace. Prepare each row separately.

Materials required
- *roughly 1.5m (4ft 11in) nylon thread for each necklace row*
- *bugles, round small glass beads (3mm (¹⁄₈in) in diameter) in matching colours*
- *glue*
- *2 bead tips*
- *1 clasp*

❶ Preparing the rows
Thread two bugles and one round small glass bead on to the nylon thread and go back through the two bugles.

❷ Repeat this process at 2cm (³⁄₄in) intervals, varying the number of bugles you use between one and four to make pendants of different lengths. Complete all the rows using the same technique.

❸ Assembly
Tie all the rows together at both ends with a tight double knot, add a dab of glue and insert into the bead tips. Attach the bead tips to the clasps.

1. THREAD YOUR NYLON THROUGH A SMALL GLASS BEAD BEFORE GOING BACK THROUGH THE BUGLES.

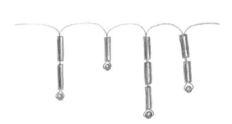

2. MAKE UP PENDANTS OF DIFFERENT LENGTHS.

3. PLACE A SMALL AMOUNT OF GLUE ON THE KNOT AND ASSEMBLE THE BEAD TIP AND CLASP.

This necklace is stretchy and will adapt to fit the natural contours of your neck.

Funky Flair

For best results, calculate the length of your necklace or bracelet then lay the beads out on a table to see how the finished effect will look. The crimp beads should be an appropriate size for the thickness of the plastic tubing.

Materials required

- roughly 50cm (20in) plastic tubing for a necklace, 20cm (8in) for a bracelet
- novelty beads and buttons in assorted colours
- crimp beads
- flat-nosed pliers
- 2 jump rings
- 2 leather crimps
- glue
- 1 clasp

1 Start from the centre of the necklace or bracelet. Thread on a crimp bead, a novelty bead and another crimp bead. Using flat-nosed pliers, gently squeeze the crimps to secure the novelty bead.

2 Working out in both directions, repeat step 1 until you reach the desired length. Space the beads roughly 2cm (³/₄in) apart. To attach the buttons, thread on one or two small beads on either side of the foot of the button and secure on both sides with a crimp.

3 Add a dab of glue to the end of the plastic tubing and place inside the leather crimp. Tighten the crimp with the flat-nosed pliers and attach to the clasp with a jump ring if necessary. Do the same for the other end of the necklace or bracelet.

1. SECURE EACH BEAD WITH TWO CRIMP BEADS.

2. SPACE YOUR BEADS AND BUTTONS AT REGULAR INTERVALS.

2A. SECURING THE BUTTONS.

3. ATTACHING THE CRIMP AND CLASP.

Delicate Trinket Threads

Materials required

- *roughly 50cm (20in) tiger tail for each necklace row, 20cm (8in) for each bracelet row*
- *novelty beads in assorted colours*
- *crimp beads*
- *flat-nosed pliers*
- *1 clasp (avoid using barrel clasps when making bracelets)*
- *glue*
- *2 bead tips*

❶ Preparing the rows
Divide the beads up into as many piles as you want rows. Lay the beads out on a table to see how the finished effect will look.

❷
Start from the centre of each row of tiger tail. Crush a crimp bead using your flat-nosed pliers, then thread on a bead and crush another crimp bead to secure.

❸
Repeat step 2, spacing the beads roughly 2cm (3/4in) apart, until you reach the required length.

❹ Assembling the clasp
To fasten a single-row necklace or bracelet, thread on a crimp bead then take the tiger tail through the ring of the clasp and back through the crimp bead. Crush the bead using the flat-nosed pliers. To fasten a multi-row necklace, thread the lengths of tiger tail through a crimp bead and crush. Trim the tiger tail roughly 1mm (1/16in) from the crimp bead. Add a dab of glue to the crimp and place in a bead tip. Attach it to the clasp. Repeat this process at the other end of the necklace or bracelet.

2. STARTING OFF.

3. THREADING ON THE BEADS.

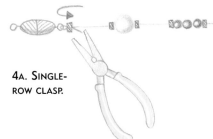

4A. SINGLE-ROW CLASP.

You can also use doubled-up bicycle brake cable as the main thread for this jewellery (see left). However, bicycle brake cable is made up of several very fine strands of metal that may cause injury if the ends are left hanging free, so take special care.

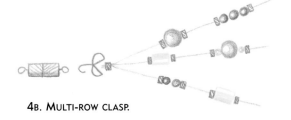

4B. MULTI-ROW CLASP.

Stardust

Materials required

- *1m (39in) tiger tail or 60cm (24in) for a short necklace*
- *1 clasp*
- *12 novelty beads*
- *crimp beads*
- *flat-nosed pliers*

① To make the necklace
Cut the tiger tail in half and attach each length to the clasps using a crimp bead (see page 6).

② Working symmetrically, thread on a crimp bead, a novelty bead and another crimp bead. Crush the crimps with flat-nosed pliers to secure. Repeat this pattern spacing the beads roughly 2cm (³/₄in) apart until you are roughly 10cm (4in) from the end of each length of tiger tail.

③ Thread the two lengths of tiger tail through the same crimp bead and crush the bead.

④ To make the medallion
Thread both lengths of tiger tail though a novelty bead and secure with a crimp bead.

⑤ To make the pendants
Thread a novelty bead on the end of each length of tiger tail and secure with crimp beads. Trim the excess wire.

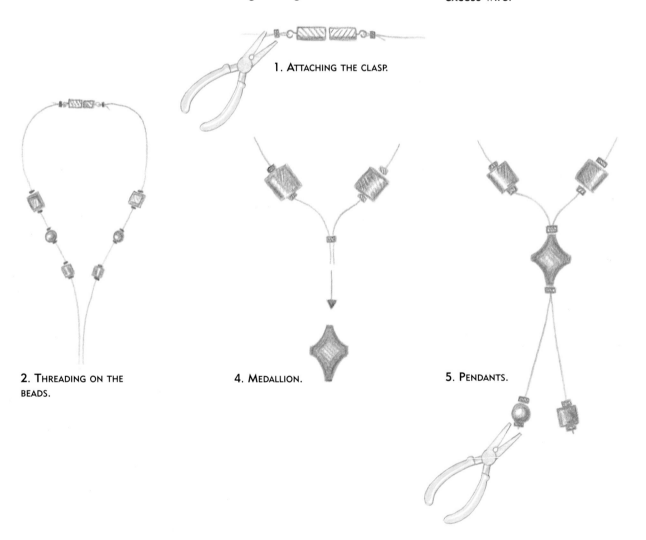

1. ATTACHING THE CLASP.

2. THREADING ON THE BEADS.

4. MEDALLION.

5. PENDANTS.

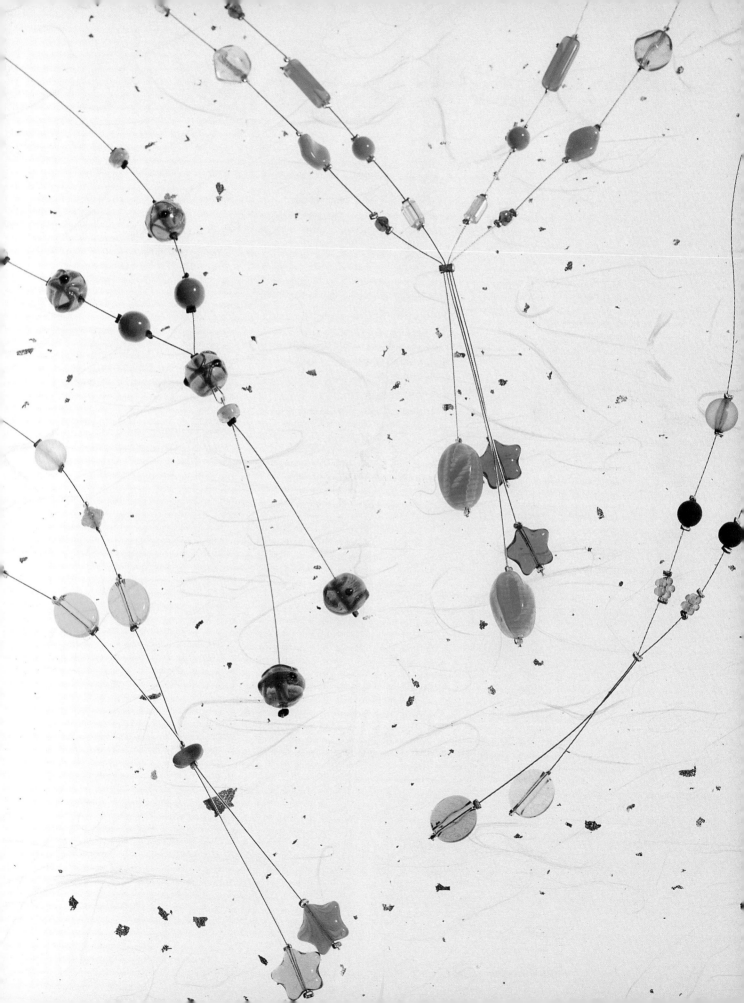

Novelty Party Necklace

Materials required
- *roughly 2m (6ft 7in) tiger tail*
- *wire cutters*
- *assorted novelty beads*
- *crimp beads*
- *flat-nosed pliers*
- *2 bead tips*
- *1 clasp*

① To make the necklace
Cut a 50cm (20in) length of tiger tail for the base wire, then cut the remaining wire into 10cm (4in) pieces.

② Thread a crimp bead, a novelty bead and another crimp bead to the centre of the base wire. Thread a 10cm (4in) length of tiger tail through these three beads, centre the short length of wire then crush the two crimp beads using the flat-nosed pliers.

③ Work outwards, repeating this process and spacing the beads roughly 5cm (2in) apart.

④ Pendants
Join each 10cm (4in) length of tiger tail to its neighbour by threading the two wires through a single novelty bead. Crush a crimp bead just under the novelty bead.

⑤ Clasp
Join the last two wires at each end of the necklace with a crimp bead. Add a dab of glue, insert the crimp into a bead tip and attach the tip to your clasp.

The necklace should end with a join between the base wire and a 10cm (4in) length. Adjust the length of the shorter piece of tiger tail to accommodate this if necessary.

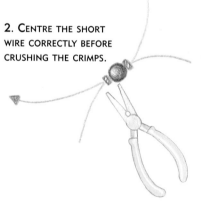

2. CENTRE THE SHORT WIRE CORRECTLY BEFORE CRUSHING THE CRIMPS.

3. SPACE THE BEADS AT REGULAR INTERVALS.

4. MAKE UP THE PENDANTS BY LINKING TWO SHORTER LENGTHS OF TIGER TAIL.

5. INSERT THE CRIMP INTO A BEAD TIP AND ATTACH THE CLASP.

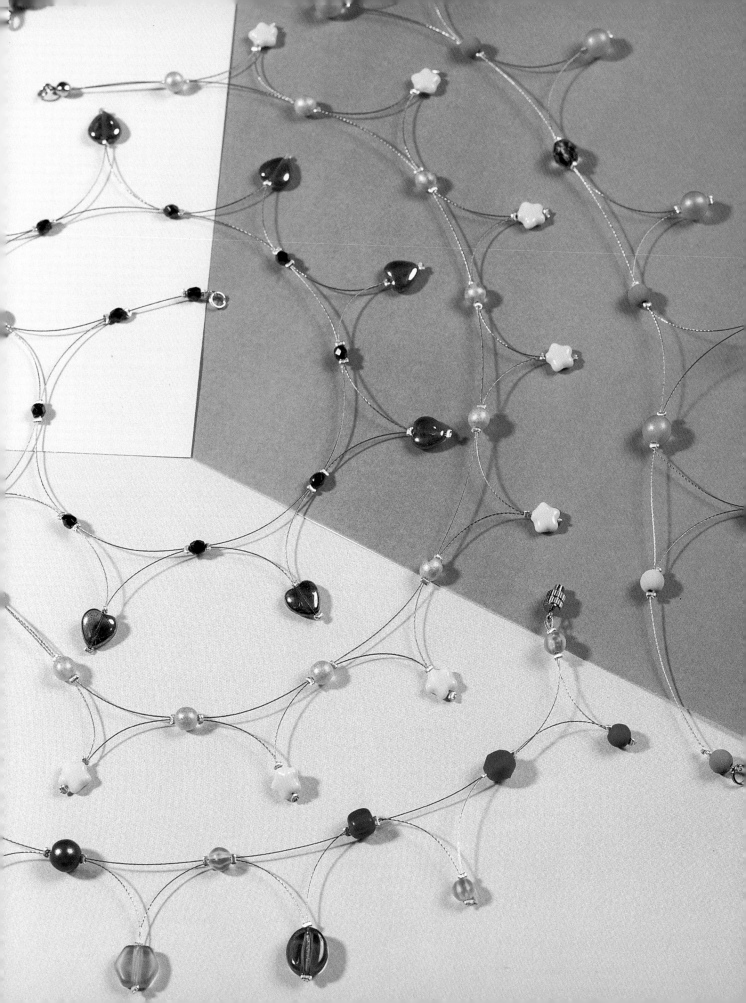

Light and Layered

You will need three to five rows to make this necklace or bracelet and several novelty beads with large openings.

Materials required

- roughly 60cm (24in) tiger tail for each necklace row, 25cm (10in) for each bracelet row
- wire cutters
- crimp beads
- glue
- 2 bead tips
- flat-nosed pliers
- 1 clasp (avoid using barrel clasps when making bracelets)
- medium-sized novelty beads in assorted colours

1 Thread all the lengths of tiger tail through the same crimp bead and crush the bead at one end of the tiger tail. Add a dab of glue and place the crimp into a bead tip. Close the bead tip and attach it to the clasp.

2 Work all the lengths of tiger tail in the same way, threading one or more novelty beads on to each wire and then threading all the wires through a crimp bead, a novelty bead and another crimp bead. Crush the two crimp beads using the flat-nosed pliers. Repeat this process until you have the desired length.

3 Repeat step 1 to attach the clasp to the other end.

1. STARTING OFF.

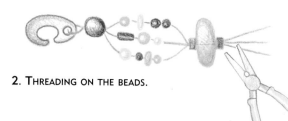

2. THREADING ON THE BEADS.

To make a more dynamic piece of jewellery try using wires of different lengths and teasing out the excess wire between the novelty bead dividers.

Drops of Sunlight

Materials required

- *roughly 2m (6ft 7in) tiger tail*
- *wire cutters*
- *crimp beads*
- *flat-nosed pliers*
- *1 clasp*
- *novelty beads in assorted colours*

1 Cut a 50cm (20in) length of tiger tail for the base wire. Cut the remaining wire into 10cm (4in) lengths.

2 Thread a crimp bead to the centre of the base wire, then thread a 10cm (4in) length of wire through. Centre the shorter wire in the crimp then crush the crimp using flat-nosed pliers.

3 Repeat this process to attach the other segments to the base wire, spacing the crimp beads roughly 5cm (2in) apart.

4 Attach the two ends of your necklace to the clasp using crimp beads (see page 6).

5 Thread a novelty bead on each short length of wire and secure at the end with a crimp bead.

2. ATTACH EACH SHORT LENGTH OF WIRE WITH A CRIMP BEAD.

3. SPACE THE CRIMP BEADS AT REGULAR INTERVALS.

4. ATTACH THE NECKLACE TO THE CLASP WITH A CRIMP BEAD.

5. ATTACH NOVELTY BEADS TO THE ENDS OF THE SHORT LENGTHS OF WIRE.

Macramé Twists

Macramé uses up a lot of thread, so to calculate the length of thread required multiply the desired length for the finished piece by eight.

Materials required
- *roughly 4m (13ft) twine or coloured string for a choker, 2m (6ft 7in) for a bracelet*
- *beads and/or holed buttons*
- *glue*

1. STARTING OFF.

① Macramé technique
Cut a length of string equal to double the length of your finished piece plus 20cm (8in). Halve this length of string (this will be your base thread) and knot the string you will use for weaving around the base thread at its midway point. Leave a small loop to fasten the jewellery (see step 4): it should be the same size as the fastening button or bead.

**② ** Pass the left string over the two base threads, and the right string over the left string and around the back of the base threads. Pull the end out through the left loop. Tighten the strings.

**③ ** Pass the right string over the base threads, then the left string over the right string and around the back of the base threads. Pull the left string out through the right loop. Tighten the threads.

**④ ** Repeat steps 2 and 3 until you have the required length. To finish, thread a bead or button on to the base threads then make up one or two macramé motifs and apply a dab of glue.

⑤ Buttons and beads
Add buttons and beads to the macramé as you go, threading them either on to the base thread or on to the macramé strings.

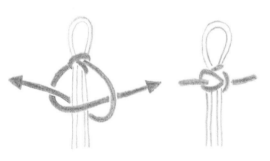

2. FIRST MOTIF.

3. SECOND MOTIF.

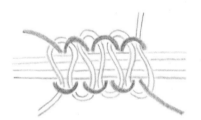

4. STANDARD MACRAMÉ.

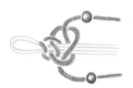

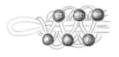

5A. BEADS ON THE MACRAMÉ STRINGS.

5B. BUTTONS ON THE MACRAMÉ STRING.

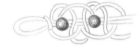

5C. BEADS ON THE BASE THREAD.

Knots and Beads

Divide the beads into as many piles as you wish to have rows and make up each row separately.

Materials required

- *roughly 1.5m (4ft 11in) string for each choker row, 50cm (20in) for each bracelet row*
- *beads and holed buttons in natural shades (including a bead or button with a large opening to hold all the threads)*
- *glue*

① Preparing the rows

Start in the centre of each row. Thread on the beads one by one or in small groups and secure them on each side with a knot. Space them 1–2cm (3/8–3/4in) apart. To thread on the buttons, work the string in pairs. Cross them on the diagonal when threading on a four-holed button, and one on top of the other for two-holed buttons. Secure the buttons with knots on each side. Make up all the rows using this technique, leaving roughly 15cm (6in) excess string at the end of each row.

② The clasp

At one end, thread all the string rows through the same bead. Fold the string back, keeping two lengths aside to secure with a herringbone knot pattern (see diagram below). Apply a small dab of glue to the knot. At the other end, make a button loop the size of the chosen bead and finish with the same herringbone knot.

1. THREADING ON THE BEADS.

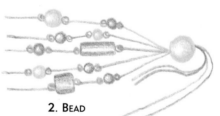

1A. ATTACHING A
TWO-HOLED BUTTON.

1B. ATTACHING A
FOUR-HOLED BUTTON.

2. BEAD
FASTENING.

BEADED END.

BUTTON LOOP END.

HERRINGBONE KNOT.